MW01288918

This journal belongs to:

••••••••••••••••••••••••••••••••••••••

A special note

Can you draw your family tree?

What were your parents like when you were a child?

What games did you play as a child?

What did you want to be growing up when you were in high school? Why?

Who is/was your best friend and what did you like to do together?

Who is/was your first love? Do you still remember him/her?

Do you have a secret talent?

What was your favorite place that you have been to?

What was your first job and how did you get it?

What do you like to do when you are free?

What was your most memorable memory as a child?

What is the happiest day of your life (so far)?

What was the strangest thing that ever happened to you?

If you could relive a day in your past, what would it be?

What were you scared of as a child but no longer now? How did you overcome it?

What school did you go to?
What was it like?

What was your favorite subject in school? Why?

What kind of games did you play in school? With who?

What sports did you play in school? How good were you at it?

What kind of student were you?

What was a typical day like when you got home from school?

Who did you admire growing up? Why?

What was the hardest thing you had to overcome so far? How did you overcome it?

What is something about you that you have never revealed to anyone else?

What do you think is the most important lesson you learnt in life? Why?

What was the most embarrassing thing that happened to you?

Do you have any big regrets in life?

What do you think is the most important thing in relationships? Why?

Who were/are your closest friends? How did you meet? What do you like most about them?

What was something your parents taught you that you still value today?

What is something children born this generation will never understand and experience?

How did you meet your life partner?

When did you know when you met 'the one'?

What were/are some family traditions that you followed?

What were/are your sibling/s like?

What were/are your grandparents like?

Who were you the closest with in your family as a child?

What were you most scared of as a child?

What are you most scared of now as an adult? Why?

What was the best present you ever received? What was your happiest memory with it?

What books did you read when you were a child?
What was your favorite?

Did you have any pets growing up?
What were their names? What did you do together?

What did you do with your first paycheck? What was your first purchase?

What was the boldest decision you made in life?

Who are you most thankful to in this world? Why?

What saying do you live by everyday? Why?

Are you happy where you are in life right now? Why?

Additional room for self-written questions

Made in the USA
Columbia, SC
26 December 2022

74994544R00061